Disclaimer

W0006849

ISBN-10: 0982743602
ISBN-13: 978-0-9827436-0-7

Fonts include Trade Gothic and ITC Officina Serif. Design by Garth Humbert and the May team.

Foreword

A lot has happened with the Customer Development process since I published *The Four Steps to the Epiphany*. When I first conceived of the concept, I was attempting to articulate a common pattern I recognized in successful startups. I did this because I wanted to change the way startups were built–without completely depending on serendipity and at a much lower cost.

Today, thousands of students have heard my lectures and more than twenty thousand have read my book on Customer Development. Hundreds, if not thousands, of startups are practicing some elements of Customer Development today. Many in the venture capital community have come to embrace the concepts, encourage and, in some cases, require their portfolio companies to adhere to the Customer Development principles.

In addition to growing adoption of Customer Development, is its advancement. A former student of mine and intrepid entrepreneur, Eric Ries, combined Customer Development with Agile development methodologies to form the powerful concept of a "Lean Startup." In little more than a year's time, there are now over 3,500 members in Lean Startup Groups in 27 cities and 9 countries. Dave McClure's AARRR metrics represent the quintessential method for measuring progress through Customer Development for web startups. In a series of deeply insightful blog posts, Ash Maurya extended my work by building a Web Startup version of Customer Development.

Before I began writing and speaking about the Customer Development model, I thought it paradoxical that these methods were employed by successful startups, yet articulated by no one. Its basic propositions were the antithesis of common wisdom yet they were followed by those who succeeded.

"It is the path that is hidden in plain sight."

No longer is it hidden. Clearly, Customer Development has lit a fire.

What I find perhaps most gratifying is this: Customer Development continues to be advanced by practitioners, mentors, entrepreneurs and investors who endeavor to build successful startups into scalable businesses. Customer Development is not one book. It's not a religion. It is a malleable, customizable, and bespoke methodology for dealing with the chaos of the real-world. And I am proud to note, it *is* growing and evolving.

This book, *The Entrepreneur's Guide to Customer Development* represents another milestone. Not only is it the first "third party" book about Customer Development, *it raises the bar*. Authors Brant Cooper and Patrick Vlaskovits have integrated the thinking of leading Customer Development practitioners and evangelists so any entrepreneur can apply them to his or her startup. They have distilled Customer Discovery into a series of steps illustrated with clear examples, concrete action items, and traps to avoid.

This is a must read for all startups and their stakeholders.

– Steven Gary Blank
Menlo Park, CA
April 2010

Acknowledgements

Without Steve Blank and his book, *The Four Steps to the Epiphany*, this book would have been, of course, impossible. Steve's shared "epiphany" of Customer Development practices and processes has inspired countless entrepreneurs, investors and other business leaders to take a hard look at the way they build new businesses. Not only do we want to thank Steve for the generous insights he has provided through his books, on his blog and in his classroom, but also for the support and encouragement he has offered us in our endeavor to write this book.

We would like to acknowledge the leading thinkers and supporters of Customer Development and its like-minded principles, specifically Eric Ries, Sean Ellis, Dave McClure and Andrew Chen. We would also like to thank those big-brained entrepreneurs and practitioners who continue to discuss and debate these ideas on Rich Collins' Lean Startup Circle Google group and elsewhere. Most importantly, these individuals put their ideas into action, share their experiences, and advance the Customer Development discipline vigorously: Ash Maurya, Babak Nivi, Cindy Alvarez, Dan Martell, David Binetti, Giff Constable, Kent Beck, Kevin DeWalt, Rich Collins and Sean Murphy. Discussing the day-to-day tactics with these people as they implement Customer Development practices has been instrumental to our own thinking reflected in this book.

Further, thanks to the following individuals for participating in our Customer Development efforts on the book and for providing valuable feedback: Adam Harris, Ann Miura-Ko, Anne Rozinat, Ash, Giff, Bill Earner, Dave Concannon, Jeff Widman, Kevin Donaldson, Kyle Matthews, Matthew Gratt, and Pete Mannix.

We would like to single out Hiten Shah for inspiring us to undertake this task and for providing us a constant stream of encouragement, contacts, and wisdom.

Finally, we would like to thank Fabrice Grinda, Bruce Moeller, Ranjith Kumaran and Jeff Smith for sharing their stories with us.

— Brant Cooper and Patrick Vlaskovits

Table of Contents

Why this book?

Steve Blank's book, *The Four Steps to the Epiphany*, changes the game. In a business world full of marketing "fluff," "get-rich-quick", self-help guides and analytical tomes that predict history with undeniable accuracy, Blank's book lays out an actionable framework for starting and building new startups, based on the insight that **most startups fail because they didn't develop their market, not because they didn't develop their product.**

Steve Blank published *The Four Steps to the Epiphany* in 2005 not as a "traditional" business book, but as a compilation of lecture notes for the business school classes he taught at Stanford University and UC Berkeley. Tens of thousands of people have purchased this "non-marketed" book. Its dog-eared pages, highlighter-marked paragraphs and note-filled margins prove its value like few other books because it doesn't get put away – it remains on the desk, never quite reaching the bookshelf.

The Four Steps to the Epiphany (referred to as *The Four Steps* throughout this book) is not a grand, conquer-the-world strategy, or a set of "tried and true" tactics, or collection of catchy business aphorisms. It is a malleable process of testing, learning and iterating upon the fundamental business assumptions you hold about your product, customers and market.

So, then, why this book? The objective of this "non-fiction novella" is to remove the barriers to understanding and implementing Customer Development (referred to as CustDev throughout this book) and take *The Four Steps* to another level. We hope to provide the following insights:

1. "Boil the content down" to an even simpler, more straightforward, actionable guide to CustDev practices.
2. Summarize and unite the ideas of modern CustDev "thought leaders" who have emerged since The Four Steps was published.
3. Put a "stake in the ground" to create standards with respect to common CustDev terms and concepts.
4. Demonstrate the flexibility of CustDev when applied to any business model.
5. Make the CustDev process available in an ebook format.

We have made it our goal to **get to the point**, but also **not get to the wrong point**. While debate is healthy, and we can only hope that people will discuss this book, we hope to minimize "paralysis by analysis." Participation in debates over terminology, semantics, or history - particularly in high-tech culture - often is an excuse for *not taking action*. We feel Customer Development does not need to be at the center of such a debate. You can, of course, take it or leave it. But more to the point, you can further it, change it, and even mold it to your business, your vision, and your values.

As Steve Blank says, "Customer Development is not just one idea, but the sum of Customer Development itself. It's more than one smart guy sitting on the beach in Hawaii writing a business book. It is what it preaches."

Who Should Read This

The Customer Development framework is not tied to a particular business type, market segment, or product category. Company size, revenues, or location are immaterial, as long as the company is planning on launching a new product.

Anyone can benefit from Customer Development thinking. The philosophy applies to all entrepreneurs even though specific Customer Development processes are typically associated with those businesses just "starting up."

Although our background is working with high-tech companies and that has formed our primary frame of reference, the Customer Development model is broad and flexible, and can be applied to various industries and markets. This book focuses on the first step of Customer Development, namely Customer Discovery. Therefore, we will focus on startups.

The reality is that Customer Development methods become more difficult to implement the "further along" your business has been established. The further along you are, the more difficult it is to question and test fundamental business assumptions upon which you may have already built an organization. If, for example, you must report revenue growth to your investors next month, it may be a difficult proposition to stop what you're doing in order to question your fundamental business assumptions. Even though taking a "time-out" to go through a set of processes that might explain why your growth is slower than projected might be exactly what you need, your board is likely to think you took the wrong turn at Albuquerque and ended up in Taos! Such a drastic step typically requires a little bit of desperation and a lot of sympathetic Directors. It might even be said, that The Four Steps was born out of just such a predicament.

Regardless of the stage your business is in, those of you most likely to pick up this book are significantly involved in a startup technology company, either as a developer, product manager, or founder. Fundamentally, this is a book for entrepreneurs who are willing and able to question their most tightly-held business assumptions; it is for this group of people this book will benefit the most.

"[SuperMac was] one of the first companies to sell an external disk drive for the original Mac; they had the first 'color paint programs' for the Mac; and when the Mac was just black and white they had the first color graphics boards and large screen color monitors for the Mac. And with all of that they had gone broke, out of business and into Chapter 11... no one inside the company had a profound belief in who the company was and why they existed. They had no model of who their own customers were and what it would take to make those customers bang down their doors to buy their products.

Nothing I couldn't fix. I took the job."

– Steven Blank

In *The Four Steps*, Steve recognizes specific cases where CustDev may be inappropriate. Some businesses face technology risk, but little or no market risk. Steve Blank states that:

> "the risk in biotechnology companies is in the front-end of Product Development; [in] taking a research hypothesis and developing [it] into a successful and effective drug, not in the back-end of customer acceptance and adoption."

Another example when CustDev may be inappropriate is in a bubble - when investors or capital markets are throwing money at any startup with "a pulse". In such instances, Steve recommends "throwing Customer Development out the window." We would caution, however, that rather than defenestrating Customer Development altogether, you may want to keep it on the shelf. Bubbles, by definition, are short-lived.

What Customer Development is

Customer Development is a four-step framework to discover and validate that you have identified the market for your product, built the right product features that solve customers' needs, tested the correct methods for acquiring and converting customers, and deployed the right resources to scale the business.

At an abstract level, Customer Development is simply about questioning your core business assumptions. It applies an engineering, or scientific method, to what is really not a scientific endeavor (building a business). Your process will resemble the scientific method by following these steps:

- Observing and describing a phenomenon
- Formulating a causal hypothesis to explain the phenomenon
- Using a hypothesis to predict the results of new observations
- Measuring prediction performance based on experimental tests

This process is used to discover and validate the following business-related information:

- A product solves a problem for an identifiable group of users (Customer Discovery)
- The market is saleable and large enough that a viable business might be built (Customer Validation)
- The business is scalable through a repeatable sales and marketing roadmap (Company Creation)
- Company departments and operational processes are created to support scale (Company Building)

There's an old sales adage that says "maybe" is the worst answer you can get from a customer. This applies to Customer Development as well. The first desired outcome of implementing Customer Development is a thriving, successful company; all Customer Development can promise is to maximize the potential to succeed.

The second most desired outcome is the realization that there is no market, or that the market is insufficient upon which to build the business you desire. The iterative aspect of Customer Development is designed to eliminate the middle ground between these two end points. At each phase gate, you "pivot" - change your assumption(s) - in order to test another path. Ultimately, you either find the path, or realize that the market has spoken and close the business.

Customer Development

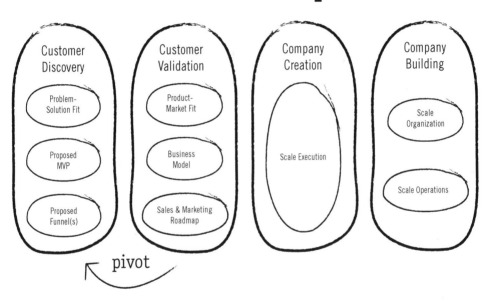

Figure 1: Steven Blank's Four Steps of Customer Development

What Customer Development is Not

Customer Development is neither a rigid set of actions that leads to business success, nor is it a "high-falutin'" philosophy that requires deep contemplation and adherence to laws brought down from "nigh", lest you be cast away into startup hell. To wit, Customer Development is neither authoritative nor dogmatic.

Customer Development grew out of Steve Blank's experience: "distilled from things I got right, and things I screwed up," as well as by his observations of the practices of successful companies.

Successful implementation of Customer Development, let alone simply believing in it, will not guarantee success for your business. Customer Development will help you – force you – to make better decisions based on tested hypotheses, rather than untested assumptions. The results of the Customer Development process may indicate that the assumptions about your product, your customers and your market are all wrong. In fact, they probably will. And then it is your responsibility, as the idea-generator (read: entrepreneur), to interpret the data you have elicited and modify your next set of assumptions to iterate upon.

Many "airport business books" urge entrepreneurs to never give in. They tell them to persist in their dream of building a great product and/or company, no matter what the odds are or what the market might be telling them – success is just around the corner. They tend to illustrate this sort of advice with inspiring stories of entrepreneurs who succeeded against all odds and simply refused to throw in the towel. While maintaining persistence and willpower is certainly good advice, Customer Development methodologies are designed to give you data and feedback you may not want to hear. It is incumbent upon you to listen. There are no billion-dollar companies who will proclaim to you that Customer Development was the model they used to achieve success. On the other hand, most billion-dollar companies have practiced some element of Customer Development, regardless of whether they knew what it was or what they may have called it.

Three Levels of Learning

There are three levels to discussing Customer Development:

1. Understanding the philosophy.
2. Applying the principals to your specific business.
3. Laying out the concrete steps to take.

Philosophy
If you put down this book having learned only one thing, we hope that it would be simply this: **"Question Your Assumptions"**.

Separate the zeal of entrepreneurship from the blindness of hubris. Pivot your way to achieving your vision or let the market guide you to a different conclusion. Most successful companies have done this.

Principles
Applying CustDev principles to your specific business is perhaps the toughest task you will face. If you have a simple business model, you're likely good-to-go. Testing your assumptions regarding the right product for the right customer, how to best deliver the product, and how to most efficiently reach and convert your customers is a fairly straightforward process. But the more complex your model and your business ecosystem, the more difficult it is to figure out the order in which to test assumptions, who to test them against, and how. There are no right or wrong answers, but as you dig deeper into all the variables you must evaluate, you will realize how high your "house of cards" actually is.

The Steps
If you can navigate how to apply these principles to your business model successfully, working through the actual steps outlined in this book will be relatively easy to understand, if not surprisingly difficult to implement. Hopefully our exercises and "pitfalls to avoid" will help you navigate through the obstacles encountered when actually getting out and doing it.

Getting Started

Customer Development, as a framework, must be tailored to your business. In order to help you accomplish this goal, we have structured this book as follows:

- We provide you with our interpretation of key concepts and definitions related to marketing, Customer Development, and "Lean Startups"
- Next, we help you "describe" your business, including your vision, model, product and target market, in a way that prepares you for Customer Development
- Finally, we provide you with the steps to take in order to complete the first step of Customer Development: Customer Discovery

Future books will attempt to tackle other portions of the Customer Development process - believe us when we say that Customer Discovery is more than enough to "bite off" at one time.

Naïve Thinking

SonicMule makes mobile products for a new phenomenon called "social music." While SonicMule founders Jeff Smith and Dr. Ge Wang's vision of their business was clear, how to actually realize it was anything but. We spoke with CEO Jeff Smith about how their diligence toward testing turns guesses into facts.

As we were setting up for the interview, we were chatting about our own music playing, which dovetailed into our formal conversation:

Author: My own music playing, regardless of my skill or lack thereof, is about playing with my brothers.

Jeff: Before recording was invented, all music was about playing and usually socially. The philosophy of our company, the vision for us is that music is a social experience. Music, today, is ripe for being redefined - and by redefined I really mean being returned back to its roots as a social experience.

Author: So that's a really big vision - where do you start?

Jeff: Well, we knew we wanted to go mobile, but being a B2B enterprise software guy, what did I know? So we approached the market with "naive thinking", which means we would have to test a theory and iterate and test again and that's how we have gone at it since day one. Test if the technology works, if the distribution works, if there's a value proposition.

Author: It seems that you have built a slew of products in a short period of time. Were you searching for the right application?

Jeff: We developed specific "mini products", each of which tested different components. Actually, the first thing we built was a mobile analytics engine that would allow us to figure out exactly what people were doing with the products and why. And as we got users, we interacted directly with them in order to calibrate some of the data we were getting out of the analytics. Later, it helped us calibrate our research of marketing conversions.

But the very first product we built was a virtual cigarette lighter for the iPhone. It was cool. The flame was rendered at 30 frames per second and you could play with the flame; you could blow it out. Our feeling was that if you didn't get to the demo within thirty seconds, forget about it. So, blowing out the flame became a classic word of mouth demo. In fact, you could click on the world and see where other people were igniting their flames at that point in time. It was this crazy social experience around awareness, but the whole point of the exercise was to see if some of these pieces of functionality would work - the technology to simulate blowing out the flame, the viral distribution. The product was a great success, though we found only 3% of our users igniting one phone to another.

Author: And 3% wasn't going to cut it...

Jeff: Right, so we did a course correction half way into Tech Boom to improve that number and when we launched Tech Boom, a virtual fire cracker to test if people would do phone-to-phone networking (over sound), that number was up to 20%.

The next day I came in to work and said if we don't have a latency problem on the phone, it would open up a whole dimension of what our value proposition could be. The next day we launched Sonic Vox, which allows you to turn your voice into Darth Vader in real-time. This was a one-day application.

Three weeks later, we launched Ocarina to test whether we could move sonic networking from an impersonal state, as in igniting one phone with another, to a personally self-expressive state through the creation and sharing of Ocarina songs.

Author: A huge percentage of iPhone applications are free. Did you go with a free or paid model?

Jeff: All of our apps required payment from the beginning. This was the only way we felt we could truly test our value proposition. We're now up to 4M paid users.

Author: How does this become really big? Are you in search of a business model that makes you a truly scalable business?

Jeff: We're not out of the woods yet, there are still questions we need answers to. But we're pretty confident about the future of social music. What we found is:

1. Everyone cares about social music
2. It's fantastic from a marketing standpoint because it puts our users to work for us. We believe the data is in, this is real, so we're doubling down.

Author: So you've tested and proven the technology, tested and proven there's a potentially huge market, tested and optimized appropriate channels, and are now in the test and iterate the business model phase.

Jeff: Yes. We did much more testing on market channels in the second half of '09. Now we are moving on to business model and engagement. We are expanding the model to better monetize our base of 4M users. How do we increase monetization per user? Can we open up social music capability to partners?

Concept Definitions

Early Adopters/Earlyvangelists

Segmentation

Market Type

"Non-Traditional" Business Models

Positioning

Product-Market Fit

Minimum Viable Product (MVP)

Pivot

Getting Out of the Building

For each of the definitions, we draw upon our knowledge from a "Customer Development" context. We have not studied Japanese lean manufacturing (Kaizen); we didn't search for the original source of the term "Minimum Viable Product;" we didn't interview Mark Andreessen about Product-Market Fit. Our intent here is to synthesize recent thinking on these subjects and "put a stake in the ground" as to what these terms mean in today's startup community. You may not agree with our definition of a concept, but at least you'll know what we mean when we use one of the terms. You can argue whether a particular tactic is "lean" or is "not lean," but be forewarned, we're going to interpret that as an excuse to avoid "getting out of the building."

Early Adopters/ Earlyvangelists

In a Nutshell: *Passionate, early users of new technology or products who understand its value before mainstream markets. Acquiring early adopters is important to jumpstart product adoption.*

Geoffrey Moore, in his 1992 book *Crossing the Chasm* adapted and popularized the concept of the "Technology Life Cycle Adoption Curve," whereby technology is adopted in five phases categorized by the type of buyer:

- **Innovators** – aggressively pursue new technology, often out of pure interest in technology.

- **Early adopters** – are the first to pursue technology for its intrinsic benefits.

- **Early majority** – rely on benefits of new technology, but will wait for others to work out the kinks.

- **Late majority** – not interested in technology per se; waits for established leader to emerge, buys de facto standard.

- **Laggards** – don't want anything to do with technology; uses technology when it's without knowledge of its existence.

The movement to each phase is hindered by a gap caused by the difference between a product's requirements and the buying habits of customers from the subsequent phase. Moore's book concentrates on the gap between early adopters and the early majority - a gap that is so wide and deep, it's best described as a chasm. CustDev concentrates on getting to and preparing to cross the chasm.

The Revised Technology Adoption Life Cycle

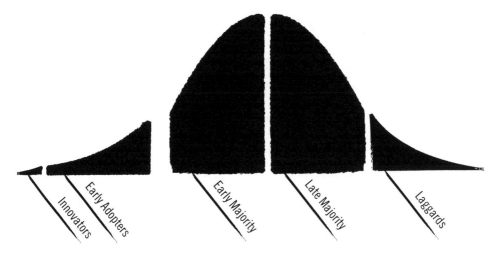

Figure 2: Moore's Revised Technology Adoption Life Cycle Curve

Early adopters are important to startup companies because they:

- Seek out new technology to solve their (or their companies') problems, not just for the sake of owning the newest technology.

- Don't rely on references from others to make buying decisions. While they are influenced by other early adopters, their main concern is solving a known problem.

- Early Adopters want to help you and (here is the best bit) want you to be successful. Early adopters enjoy opportunities that allow them to be heroes, by solving real problems.

Segmentation

In a Nutshell: *The practice of breaking down a larger market into smaller identifiable group of users who share specific needs and who reference each other.*

Market segmentation is often confused with customer profile or industry verticals. The definition is a bit more sophisticated: Market segments are comprised of like people, who share a common interest, **who have access to each other and who look to one another as a trusted reference**. If a customer prospect in California shares a need with a prospect in Zaire, **but they do not share a means of communication**, they are in separate segments. Similarly, if both prospects are in New York, but work in very different industries and have different responsibilities, they are likely to be in different segments. You treat them that way, because typically, your marketing and sales must target each differently.

The point isn't that the individuals within a segment do communicate with each other, but rather that they "have access" to do so.

The reasoning is:

1. Word of mouth regarding products works best among those who share a need and a means to communicate a solution.
2. "Access to each other" indicates a common methodology to reach them.
3. Indirect knowledge (e.g., PR, testimonials, etc.) of like individuals buying a product is a powerful influence.

One of the basic tenets of Moore's *Crossing the Chasm* is that one should choose one segment with which you establish a "beachhead on the shores" of the early majority. Attempting to scale a business when forced to customize products, tailor marketing activities and execute sales processes for multiple segments is a difficult proposition.

While targeting multiple segments is less expensive today in terms of development costs and marketing efficiency, sticking to the "one segment" philosophy maximizes the benefits of segmentation. Proper segmentation allows you to:

- Learn faster about market fit
- Find an "unoccupied" segment, i.e., no competition
- Become a market leader earlier (by dominating a segment)
- Line up (and knock down) segments like bowling pins (one segment conquered successfully destabilizes its neighbors)
- Maximize capital efficiency by focusing existing resources

Fortunately, one of the big benefits of Internet marketing, especially social media, is that it may allow you to pick up neighboring segments opportunistically, while you remain dedicated to building value for your core constituency.

Market Type

In a Nutshell: *A concept coined by Steve Blank to describe different types of market conditions confronting new products, comprised of existing market, re-segmented market, and new market.*

If you are introducing a new product into a new market:

- Your technology is so dramatically new that the existing market is shattered.
- By definition, your product owns 100% market share.
- You must explain to your customers what the product is, what it's for, and how they will use it.
- Your target users will likely NOT stop using a product when they start using yours, because no other products exist in the market. If they do stop using a product, it is one that is being replaced with a completely new product type, not a new product of the same (or similar) type. For example, the automobile replaced the horse-drawn carriage.

Existing market
A new product entering an existing market is primarily attempting to steal market share from major market players. The new product isn't trying to grow the market "pie," as much as steal a "slice."

In this market type, users will stop using a competitor's product to use yours. They will use your product because it has compelling features and better product functionality, not because you are offering a dramatically lower price to a targeted group of price-sensitive users, or a specific set of functionality toward a group of users with unique needs.

Re-segmented existing market (low cost and niche)
A new product entering an existing market with a sustainable, dramatically lower price, not only takes market share from incumbents, but expands the size of the market by selling to price-sensitive customers who otherwise do not purchase from anyone. Either customers will stop using a competitors' product and use yours because of significant cost savings or they will simply start using yours because they could not afford to use your competitors'.

33

Similarly, a new product entering an existing market with unique functionality targeted at a specific user class, not only takes market share from incumbents, but expands the size of the market by selling to new customers brought to the market by the new functionality. Either customers will stop using a competitors' product and use yours because your functionality better matches their needs, or you will acquire new users because existing products never adequately fit their needs.

"Rules of Thumb"

The toughest distinction to make is whether your product represents a new market, or is re-segmenting an existing market. There is a tendency for startup entrepreneurs to believe that they have a new product for a new market, though this is rarely the case. It can be argued that most technological advances either lower costs or enable new functionality that improves problem resolution within existing markets. True market disruption often requires major technology innovation or uses existing technology in a new and unforeseen way. **Most likely, you are re-segmenting a market.**

Further, here are two seemingly paradoxical points to consider:

1. Your customers' view of your market type is more important than yours.

2. You can choose your market type.

First, you can say that you are in a particular market type, existing in a particular place with respect to competitors within a specified market, but if the customer doesn't see it that way, what good are your beliefs? For example, if you develop "Facebook for senior citizens," you and your techy friends, as well as tech savvy pundits will see that you have segmented the social networking market for the senior citizens' market niche. All well and good, but if the senior citizens have never heard of Facebook, what good does the comparison do you? Try a landing page headline proclaiming your product as the "Facebook for Seniors" with this group and see how far it gets you.

Second, if you don't have a lot of money, you need to act like you are re-segmenting a market. Launching in a new market requires millions of marketing dollars to teach customers what the new product does and why they need it. Launching in an existing market also requires millions of marketing dollars to compete with the existing players who hope to squash you. If you don't have millions of dollars to spend, you must build your business or prove the traction to investors by dominating a specific niche market segment. In the latter case, you are essentially in a "segmented new market" that acts in a similar way to a re-segmented existing market.

"Non-Traditional" Business Models

In a Nutshell: *Business models that do not sell a product to a customer directly for a set amount of money. For example, business models that include some element of "free" or the desire to demonstrate scale prior to revenue.*

Later on, we will discuss how to apply Customer Development processes to "alternative" business models. First we wanted to make a clear distinction between the terms. It's important to distinguish between entrepreneurs who believe that free is the best way to grow their businesses, versus those who are reluctant to test the validity of their ideas with the ultimate market arbiter - cold hard cash. The two are not (necessarily) the same.

Freemium businesses are those that offer multiple account levels differentiated on product functionality and price, one of which is free. A freemium business must have one version or account level that requires payment. Otherwise, by definition, it is free, not freemium.

A "free" business model is used by a business when its primary early objective is user-growth, prior to knowing (as opposed to assuming to know) how to monetize the users through ad revenues, selling leads, meta-data, or virtual goods. Some of these businesses may be "pre-revenue model". For example, they haven't decided the exact method they will use to monetize the users. Some businesses need the free usage of one product in order to sell those users other goods, while others require the number of users to scale (up) before a value creation mechanism kicks in.

Positioning

In a Nutshell: *Positioning is the act of placing your product within a market landscape, in your audience's mind.*

In Geoffrey Moore's Crossing the Chasm, product positioning includes the following insights: knowing who your customers are and their needs; the name of your product and its product type or category; what the key benefit of the product is to your customer (the compelling reason to buy); the "state of being" without your product; and how your product differs or "changes the game."

Your positioning will form the basis of your communications with all of your constituents, including customers, investors, partners, employees, etc. For your customer, the goal of positioning is to have them understand what benefit they will receive from you and why you are better than everyone else.

Notes:
Your **differentiator** is not your compelling reason to buy, but **the benefit** the differentiator provides, likely is. So, for example, if you are the first to offer a sales force automation tool in a SaaS business model, your customers don't buy **because** you are SaaS, though this is your primary differentiator. They buy because of the benefits that SaaS provides outweigh the benefits that an in-source solution provides: IT costs are lower; deployment costs are lower; remote access is easier; integration with the web is easier; web interface lowers training costs, etc.

Your positioning varies by audience. In the example from the Market Type discussion, "Facebook for Seniors" is bad positioning for your customer, but perhaps very appropriate for investors, partners, and some media and analysts. This leads us to issue a note of caution when briefing media (PR) and analysts (AR) too early: wrong positioning (and untimely PR) can kill your company. If you are branded by media and analysts in a way that confuses customers or lumps you with existing products incorrectly, you may never be able to undo the damage.

Product-Market Fit

In a Nutshell: *When a product shows strong demand by passionate users representing a sizable market.*

Mark Andreessen defines Product-Market fit as "being in a good market with a product that can satisfy that market." Steve Blank writes that "Customer Validation proves that you have found a set of customers and a market who react positively to the product: By relieving those customers of some of their money." In a traditional business model - one in which products are sold for money - Product-Market Fit requires three criteria be satisfied:

1. The customer is willing to pay for the product.
2. The cost of acquiring the customer is less than what they pay for the product.
3. There's sufficient evidence indicating the market is large enough to support the business.

All businesses need to reach revenue at some point, so all businesses must have a Product-Market fit milestone. If you cannot prove that you can acquire customers for less than what you earn from selling them your product, you have a fundamental business problem. While the Product-Market fit definition may seem rather obvious, and getting to revenue is a clear milestone, measuring Product-Market fit from a market acceptance perspective is a bit more difficult.

Sean Ellis offers this view: "achieving Product-Market fit requires at least 40% of users saying they would be "very disappointed" without your product. Admittedly this threshold is a bit arbitrary, but I defined it after comparing results across nearly 100 startups. Those that struggle for traction are always under 40%, while most that gain strong traction exceed 40%."

Of course, it is possible to build a successful business with less than half of your customers being very disappointed without it. I'm sure you can think of many products you buy that you could easily live without. Conversely, not all businesses with greater than 40% will succeed. But here's why 40-50% is a reasonable number - first, if you buy into Moore's technology lifecycle adoption curve, your target customer at this point is the early adopter. Your early adopter will care significantly more about your product than the early majority or late majority adopters will. Second, if you have waited to try and scale your business until achieving that mark (as Ellis recommends), then you want to be sure you have **nailed it** before you spend money on demand creation efforts (scaling up).

While the 40% number is a good indication that you have achieved Product-Market fit, it doesn't say anything about the **size of the market**. Does that matter? The answer depends on your values and funding desires (discussed in the next section). Regardless, a bottoms-up approach to market sizing at this point should be quite straightforward, since you know a lot about your market segment and likely, other segments you could eventually target to grow the market. As Sean Ellis says, "crazy startups pivot away from strong customer-perceived value in search of a bigger market." But that doesn't mean you shouldn't think through where a particular segment is taking you from a scaling point of view.

Finally, even if you are lucky enough to have such strong evidence, this doesn't necessarily mean 1) it will last; 2) the size of the market is large enough to sustain the type of business you hope to build. As Ben Horowitz points out[1], often the evidence is not so clear, and even it is, it may not be where you end up.

[1] http://bit.ly/BenHorowitz

Minimum Viable Product (MVP)

In a Nutshell: *A product with the fewest number of features needed to achieve a specific objective, and users are willing to "pay" in some form of a scarce resource.*

So all our efforts to "not be too academic" failed with that nutshell definition, but read on.

Eric Ries' original definition is "the minimum viable product is that version of a new product which allows a team to collect the maximum amount of validated learning about customers with the least effort." This definition has evolved over time, but its essence has not changed much from Steve Blank's product feature set hypothesis in the Customer Discovery phase of *The Four Steps*: "the last part of your customer/problem brief is one that the Product Development team will be surprised to see. You want to understand the smallest feature set customers will pay for in the first release."

We've purposefully generalized the definition to avoid "money" as part of the definition since it's possible to define "intermediate" MVPs that not only measure something useful ("validate learning"), but also act to *minimize risk* while on route to discovering the correct business model. Incorporating some element of supply and demand, however, is important to ensure you are measuring something that matters. Think of an MVP as requiring a trade of some scarce resource (time, money, attention) for the use of the product, such that the transaction demonstrates the product might be useful or even successful, i.e., viable. For non-paying milestones, you must define the currency and your objective (what you are trying to learn). For example, intermediate MVPs might include: landing page views that prove there's some amount of interest in a product; a time commitment for an in-person meeting to view a demo that shows the customer's problem being resolved; or a resource commitment for a pilot program to test how the product fits into a particular environment.

While there's little disagreement that a business should move "to revenue" as quickly as possible, the MVP evolves through the stages between product conception and Product-Market fit. As Eric says, "that's why entrepreneurship in a lean startup is really a series of MVP's, each designed to answer a specific question (hypothesis)." Both "a landing page and a buy button"[1] and a working hardware prototype can be considered MVPs, depending on the product, market, and current objective of the product owner.

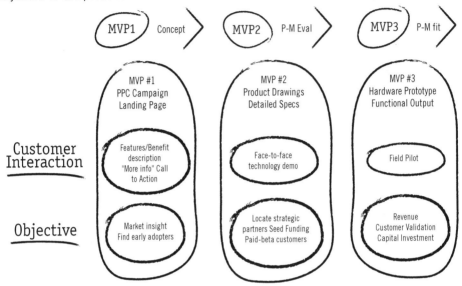

Figure 3: Example MVP Evolution

Figure 3 demonstrates an example of the MVP evolution for a new, miniaturized 3-D video camera:

All three columns are valid MVPs designed to move the company along the path of Customer Development, from concept through to paid product. Founder decides to test market viability through a landing page that describes the proposed product, technology, features and benefits. The objective is to get users to click on a specific "call to action." The currency, in MVP1, is "attention" or "interest." MVP2 includes a mishmash of technical specifications, detailed drawings and perhaps the ability to demonstrate key technology. Depending on the audience, the founder's objective may be to win investment, technology partnership, or committed beta customers. The final MVP is an early version of the product that is not necessarily in its final form factor, but that is actually usable by customers to solve a real problem. The currency at this stage is most assuredly Greenback.

Note that in this context "viable" is not **limited** by an external determination of success, but rather is framed by the entrepreneur's objective (user scale, specific functionality, payment) as measured by specific "currency" (usage, problem solved, money).

Lean Startup

In a Nutshell: *A startup which combines fast, iterative development methodologies with customer development principles.*

A concept coined (and trademarked) by Eric Ries, a Lean Startup is one that combines fast-release, iterative development methodologies (e.g., Agile) with Steve Blank's "Customer Development" concepts. Eric writes that lean startups are born out of three trends:

- The use of platforms enabled by open source and free software
- The application of agile development methodologies
- Ferocious customer-centric rapid iteration, as exemplified by the Customer Development process

We would add a fourth element, and that is the use of powerful, low-cost, and easy-to-use analytics. While some characteristics of lean startups have been practiced for years, the confluence of these trends is a recent phenomenon and offers the **potential** for unprecedented "speed of iteration," or "number of learning cycles per dollar," as a business hones in on product-market fit.

Figure 4 demonstrates that customer development and product development are two distinct, but interrelated and iterative processes. As Eric Ries describes[1], the Customer Development team works on testing the assumptions about who the customers is, the problem they hope to solve, and what the solution should be, while the Product Development team actually builds the solution. The Product Development process receives input from customers indirectly through Customer Development, and (when available) by measuring product use directly. The Product Development process iterates on the product continuously, releasing new or different functionality directly to the customer as quickly as possible.

[1] http://bit.ly/EricRiesPivot

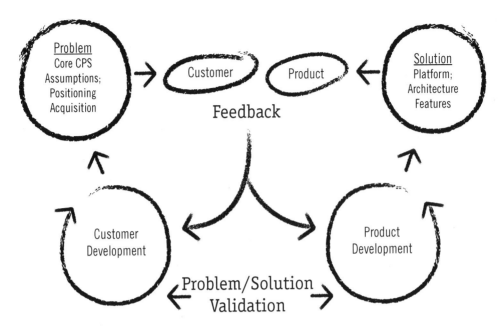

Figure 4: Lean Startup: Customer and Product Development Interrelatedness

The Customer Development process receives input from customers indirectly through Product Development reports about feature usage, but also directly from Customer Development processes and analytics. The Customer Development process iterates on core business assumptions, product functionality, and acquisition and conversion assumptions, resulting in updated hypotheses, honed messaging, positioning, feature requirements, and marketing and sales tactics.

In the Customer Discovery context, a lean startup is **not** one that **necessarily** uses lean manufacturing precepts per se, but rather one that uses fast, iterative development practices along with Customer Development methodologies in order to:

1. Validate core hypotheses (customer-problem-solution).
2. Develop the minimum viable product.
3. Achieve Product-Market fit.
4. Produce a development and marketing roadmap for scaling.

Creating a proper iteration loop requires you to predefine success and failure for each stage and to create a means to measure your progress. For example, in the web-based world, Dave McClure's AARRR metrics[1] (Acquisition, Activation, Retention, Referral, and Revenue) can be applied to measure the testing loops inside the various ustomer and Product Development stages from concept to product-market fit (and beyond).

It is perhaps worth pointing out what criteria are **not required** in ordered to be considered **lean** in Eric Ries' context:

- Bootstrapped
- Consuming unholy amounts of Top Ramen on a daily basis
- Unpaid workers
- Build system based on a 386 architecture
- Open cubicle culture
- Command-line interface
- Chairs without casters

[1] http://bit.ly/DaveMcClureAARRR

Pivot

In the Customer Development context, pivot means to change an element(s) of your customer-problem-solution hypotheses or business model, based on learning. As Eric Ries writes "by testing, each failed hypothesis leads to a new pivot, where we change just one element of the business plan (customer segment, feature set, positioning) – but don't abandon everything we've learned."

Pivoting is at the heart of the "fail fast" concept. The sooner you realize a hypothesis is wrong, the faster you can update it and retest it.

Getting Out of the Building

This phrase is Steve Blank's short hand for not accepting your business assumptions as true. Go speak (in person, if possible) with living, breathing customers to determine the validity of your assumptions. For many people, speaking with customers is difficult to do. They will look for any excuse or rationalization not to undertake this task, such as feeling uncomfortable cold-calling or speaking on the phone with strangers. One reason for this reluctance is simply the fear of rejection. Some entrepreneurs would rather nurse their doomed prized possession – the Grand Idea – rather than learning quickly that there is no market for it. Part of the purpose of "getting out of the building" is to learn whether you have a viable business idea. If you don't, then you need to move on to something else as quickly as possible. You should remember that "getting out of the building" is designed to minimize your real and opportunity costs (what you could have been doing if not building a product no one wants).

Note that analytics, surveys, and other automated user-facing testing tools are complementary, to but not substitutes for "Getting Out of the Building."

Multiple Pivots

In 2005, Zingy was the largest mobile media company in the Americas, selling ringtones, wallpapers and games to carriers, media companies and consumers. The New York-based company had 130 employees and generated over $200 million in content sales. We spoke with Fabrice Grinda, Founder and CEO of Zingy (2001-2005), to hear about his multiple pivots in search of market traction.

Assumption 1: B2C with carrier billing

Zingy will sell directly to U.S. consumers using carrier billing.

The plan was modeled on Europe and Asia, where content companies sold ringtones and other cell phone content directly to consumers who paid with SMS or smartphone technology.

> "It was impossible to get any of the cell phone companies to give us access to either the delivery system for the content or to the billing. They didn't have open billing networks; they didn't really believe this could be big."

Assumption 2: B2C with direct pay

In an effort to maintain a direct-to-customer business model, Zingy tried credit card billing and 1-900 numbers. The customer buys the ringtone that is delivered to the phone. The carrier was bypassed completely.

> "But it's much more cumbersome to order online and to wait for the ringtone, than using a one click purchase directly on your phone or by sending a text message. Our product worked fine, but it just so happens that the complexity inherent in the billing that we introduced decreased potential volume by 99.9% relative to where it should be."

Assumption 3: B2B2C

Because customers wouldn't pay by credit card directly and carriers wouldn't open their billing system, Zingy decided to try and provide the content directly to the carriers. What started out as a relatively simple direct to consumers sales process, had become a business to business sale, requiring the navigation of a complex ecosystem with large, bureaucratic companies notorious for long sales cycles.

> "It was extremely hard to identify who to talk to and it was even harder to identify what it would take to get a deal done even if we did find them. These companies are notoriously risk-averse, each waiting for the other to make the first move."

Serendipity

Carriers wouldn't budge but Zingy made sure to be extremely present at the right trade shows and approach each and every carrier to setup additional meetings and "finally, randomly, one of the handset manufacturers called us out of the blue."

Zingy provided a small sample of content to one of Nextel's handset manufacturers, which still didn't include billing, but did have the ability to store credit card information directly on the phone. Though few customers were willing to do that, those that did bought a lot of ringtones, providing the necessary proof of consumer demand.

While this fact opened up the minds of Nextel executives, to scale the service Zingy was forced to develop all the code to integrate with Nextel's multiple billing systems. Meanwhile, Sprint caught wind of the deal and decided they wanted a sample of content, too, so Zingy turned over the content licenses they owned without any technical implementation and waited to hear back about sales.

> "We ran out of cash in the process; we had no more money to pay anything. We missed payroll for four or five months. The company almost went under just as we were building this platform for Nextel. And then a miracle happened. The first check from Sprint arrived."

One thing led to another. Zingy soon followed up the Sprint success by building the service sites for AT&T and Virgin Mobile. The sales of the company went from about 1M in 2002 to 200M to 2005.

> "What's interesting is the approach that finally succeeded: be extremely flexible and highly iterative."

To the Whiteboard

The application of Customer Development processes necessarily varies from business to business. While understanding core CustDev principles and applying them to simple business models is pretty straightforward, entrepreneurs using a complex business model within a complex ecosystem may struggle with the understanding of "how to test what, when?" The business ecosystem - the relationships between the company, its partners, customers and other players - creates complicated interdependencies that produce business risk and thereby influence the priority of the business assumptions you need to test and validate.

While the death of the business plan as a method to engage investors is a welcome development, it doesn't eliminate the need to **think through your business** – a process aided by, ironically, the writing of a business plan. Alexander Osterwalder's Business Model Generation[1] provides a comprehensive process for developing your business model and Steve Blank, along with Floodgate's Ann Miura-Ko[2], developed their own useful business model template[3].

Part of the problem with imploring entrepreneurs to write a business plan, or to go through complicated processes unearthing every business model variable one might encounter, or to go through a set of exercises in a Customer Development book for that matter, is the risk of discouraging entrepreneurs from actually "**Just Doing It**."

For the vast majority of entrepreneurs who are unfunded, getting products out there and iterating as they go is arguably a better use of time. On the other hand, thinking through your business, documenting your hypotheses, and creating a plan to mitigate risk are not bad ideas either! It might actually get you to (and through) your (inevitable if successful) pivots quicker.

We feel that mapping Customer Development to your business model should be a white board exercise. The goal here isn't to get you to document a million "facts," but rather to help you think through the critical areas of your business model. We seek to help define your ecosystem, identify risks, and prioritize business milestones necessary to discover and validate your core business. The end result is a proposed (final) MVP with intermediate milestones you should test first.

[1] http://bit.ly/BizModelBook [2] http://bit.ly/cv6t5M [3] http://bit.ly/cRdeWQ

First, draw a map of your ecosystem.

1. **The entities involved**. Draw a box or a circle representing each entity in your ecosystem. Entities include users, customers, channel partners, technical partners, strategic partners, advertisers, your customers' customers, etc. Include all entities that either provide value to you or receive value from your product. Value can be derived from money or the use of a product.

2. **Value can be direct** (what a user receives from using a product) or indirect (money an advertiser gets from product user eventually).

2. **Flow of currency**. Draw lines or otherwise show your assumptions regarding the flow of currency. Who pays whom?

3. **Product Distribution**. Show your assumptions regarding how the product moves through channel(s) to reach end users.

Questions to consider:
Are you relying on third party technology that requires a formal partnership?

Are you relying on channel partners that will help you bring the product to end-users?
If you have a "free" business model and are looking to scale users, who will you eventually earn money from?

Are you partnering with a manufacturing firm?

Will you sell data or leads to third parties?

Does your product benefit your customers' customers?

Second, define the value proposition for each player.
Each entity is only a member of the "ecosystem" if it will receive benefits by participating. For each member of the ecosystem, what benefit do they gain and what are they willing to trade in exchange? These value proposition statements will evolve into your core C-P-S (Customer-Problem-Solution) hypotheses that you test during Customer Discovery. For now, however, provide a concise description of the value you presume they will receive.

Examples:

- Users will be entertained
- Advertisers get the attention of thousands of users
- Buying influencer is happy to choose "green technology"
- Customer's customer gets highly qualified leads
- Channel able to sell services on top of product
- Customer will save money, mitigate risk, or increase market share

Third, posit a final MVP

As defined above, an MVP is "a product with the fewest number of features needed to achieve a specific objective, for which users are willing to 'pay' in some form of a scarce resource." The reason the definition is somewhat obtuse is that we wish to differentiate between a "final" MVP and one or more intermediate MVPs. Final MVPs ostensibly test the business model. Intermediate MVPs test high risk components of the business model.

To develop assumptions regarding your final MVP, think of what you need to provide to each entity with whom you have a direct relationship in order to achieve the value you identified above. What are the basic features of the product each user requires to get the ecosystem functioning? What does each entity pay - whether money, attention, resources or some other currency? Describing what your final MVP looks like establishes an end point to the Customer Discovery process.

- Currency = what the user/buyer "pays" for using the MVP
- MVP Metric = what you are measuring to determine viability
- Value Determinants = what the user/buyer requires (minimally) in order to spend their currency, such as features

Fourth, where's the risk?

The goal for laying out a path for your Customer Development efforts is to prioritize and test your gating factors. If you validate key assumptions, you have proven critically important aspects of your business model. If you hit unexpected roadblocks and points of failure, then you have increased your odds of success by catching these issues early.

Think of critical near-term risks. Does your technology represent a significant risk? In other words, can you build what you believe the market needs? If your technology is difficult or costly to produce, what market-testable milestones can you build that would result in sufficient evidence to induce you to pivot or move forward? A proof of concept? A prototype? A demo?

If your risks are predominately marketing ones, what minimum set of features will result in paying customers? Or: What minimum set of features will result in a minimum of X number of users?

Time and money risks may affect intermediate MVP decisions. If your MVP will require $XM to build, but you only have $X/1000M, an intermediate MVP might be the answer to "what must I prove in order to acquire additional funding?"

Think of dependencies. If your final MVP requires that X happen, then can you build an intermediate MVP around X? What does X depend on? If possible, go to the root of the dependencies.

Fifth, create your Value Path

Your value path is the journey of Customer Discovery that takes you from where you are today to your proposed final MVP and includes both intermediate MVPs and core assumptions to be tested. From the risk table you created, map out the set of core assumptions you need to test for each identified gating factor. For each intermediate MVP, you will likely have a set of assumptions to test through direct customer interaction, in addition to a version of the product to build and test through usage.

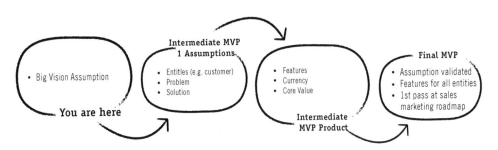

Figure 5: Value Path Template

An Example

Providing an example for this exercise is difficult. To understand the application of CustDev principles to a particular business requires a detailed understanding of the business. Deciding to delve into the business with enough detail to understand it moves your focus away from the processes themselves and toward critiquing the business. As an attempt to avoid this, we've created a (ridiculous) fictitious business.

Hopped-Up Peanut Butter (PB) is healthy "pick-you-up" energy food spread for teenagers and young adults. Made from organic peanuts and a touch of sea salt, Hopped-Up PB is also chock full of vitamins, caffeine, and taurine to give customers' energy level and brainpower a needed boost. Hopped-Up PB relies on a patented, high-energy ingredient cocktail created by a neo-Paleolithic, Hungarian peanut farmer who has agreed to issue a short term exclusive license to a pair of Australian vegemite entrepreneurs living in a Volkswagen bus at the San Elijo State Beach campground in Encinitas, California.

The Ecosystem

Hopped-Up PB wants to sell their peanut butter to U.S. moms looking for tasty, healthy, high energy food for their teen-aged sons and daughters. It is assumed that the peanut butter will be sold direct to consumers via a web-site, as well as through commercial grocery stores. Because of its "high-energy" ingredients, Hopped-Up PB will first be sold through health and fitness stores like GNC. These stores don't sell peanut butter now. The ingredient licensor has agreed to offer a short-term exclusive license to Hopped-Up PB for revenue sharing considerations in order to prove the model before a long-term contract is signed.

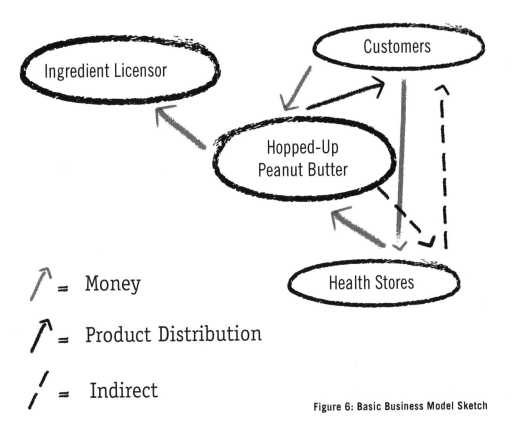

Figure 6: Basic Business Model Sketch

Value Statements

Ultimately, the licensor and the health food stores are only going to participate in this ecosystem if they make money. Health food stores also appreciate increased customer satisfaction for recurring customers and the possibility of expanding their customer base due to an exciting new product offering. Regardless of the distribution method, consumers demand high-quality and good taste, but the compelling reason (we think!) to buy is the energy boost.

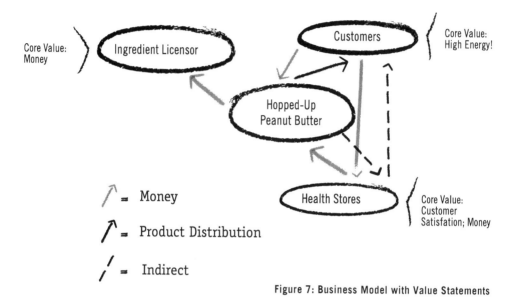

Figure 7: Business Model with Value Statements

MVP Posit

The finished MVP must deliver value to all players in the ecosystem. Because the licensor and the brick-and-mortar stores will not receive value from anything but the finished product, it is assumed both will require exactly that – the finished product. (Although advanced labeling and other brand identity collateral will not be required initially. In other words, they will require merely "Minimum Viable Packaging"). The founders have hypothesized that the minimum features required to sell Hopped Up PB are good taste and recognizable, high-quality, energy-boosting ingredients like caffeine and taurine.

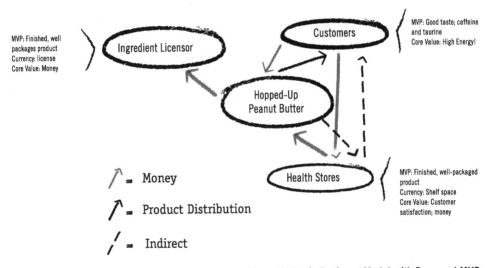

Figure 8: Basic Business Model with Proposed MVP

Risks

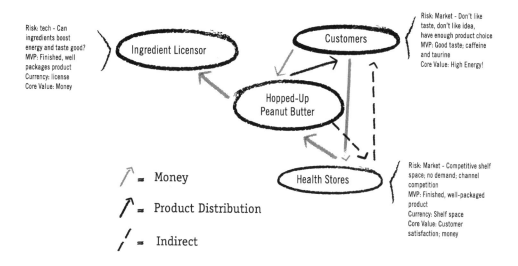

Risk: tech - Can ingredients boost energy and taste good?
MVP: Finished, well packages product
Currency: license
Core Value: Money

Risk: Market - Don't like taste, don't like idea, have enough product choice
MVP: Good taste; caffeine and taurine
Core Value: High Energy!

Ingredient Licensor

Customers

Hopped-Up Peanut Butter

Health Stores

Risk: Market - Competitive shelf space; no demand; channel competition
MVP: Finished, well-packaged product
Currency: Shelf space
Core Value: Customer satisfaction; money

↗ = Money

↗ = Product Distribution

╱ = Indirect

Risk	Type	Level	Priority	Who to Test	How to Test	Dependencies
Taste; boost	Technology	High	2	Consumers	Build product MVP	Product samples
Shelf space	Market	Med	3	Stores	Build product MVP	Complete Product
Demand	Market	High	1	Consumers	Build product MVP	none
Channel Conflict	Market	Low	4	Stores	Discounts	Complete Product

Figure 9: Basic MVP with Risk Table

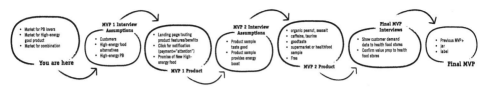

Figure 10: Business Model Value Path

Value Path

Clearly, the first item to test is whether or not a demand exists for high-energy peanut butter. Without spending a dime on the actual product, the founders could interview potential customers from various target markets, as well as set up a landing page and attempt to drive traffic and measure interest.

If that goes well, the next major milestone is to prove that the peanut butter tastes good. A full-blown product does not yet need to be produced, but rather, a way to provide free samples at health food stores.

Know thyself

As well as knowing your business, you need to take time to understand yourself. Your values will be reflected in your business and so will also affect how you conduct Customer Discovery. Do your passions align with your market segment? Is your vision reflected in your business model? Do you have strong opinions about external funding? One potential benefit of embracing Customer Development principles is that it teaches you how to be self-aware, and how to question and analyze your beliefs. It encourages you to be honest with yourself. For you to build a successful business, it is necessary to have a vision of what you hope your company will be two, three and five years down the line. The vision should be based on facts where you have them, guesses where you don't, and an honest appraisal of your business values.

Here are a few examples to get you thinking:
You might be stridently opposed to Venture Capitalist funding. That is certainly your prerogative, but you must accept the ramifications of that value. Will such a decision affect how big you can grow, and does that matter to you? Will it affect how you deal with new competitors once you have proven the attractiveness of your market? Do you still dream of building a large, publicly-traded company? Because refusing venture capital just might be at odds with that ambition.

You might be committed to serving an urban non-profit market segment, even though your Customer Discovery efforts reveal a more lucrative market segment elsewhere. This is commendable, but your vision must reflect that value and affects your Value Path.

If you require capital to grow, your vision of where the business is in five years affects the type of investment you should seek. Do you hope to have a simple Internet business that generates consistent revenue? Do you hope to build a scalable business, such as growing to at least 100M in annual revenues? We don't cast judgment on any of these businesses. They are all worthy. But the actions you take are reflected in your values and you should be realistic about what you want and formulate a corresponding strategy, while remaining flexible to what the market dictates.

On Customer-Centric Cultures

DriveCam uses video technology, expert analysis and driver coaching to save lives and reduce claims costs by improving the way people drive. We spoke with Bruce Moeller, former CEO of DriveCam (2004 - 2008) who grew the business to 50M in annual revenue, to hear how he integrated customer feedback into the company culture.

Author: You and I have talked before about an entrepreneur's need to balance customer input with the ability to stick with one's vision. You have a reputation for being adamant about listening to customers...

Moeller: To a fault (laughs). At DriveCam, we were constantly iterating based on news coming in. I had a reputation for changing the business plan every day. But seriously, if a piece of information we received from a prospective customer ran counter to what we believed to be the case, we immediately dug into the details and asked "why would they think this way?"

Author: And what about the original vision?

Moeller: I believe you have to follow where the market wants to go. In our case, the vision of the original inventor, Gary Raynor, was that the video camera was mounted in the vehicle facing outward. There were concerns about privacy (if it were to face inward), and the idea was that people would want proof if something happened to them - a recording of truth to tell your side of the story. But in reality, what we found is that people don't buy such devices before something happens; no one ever believes bad things will happen to them.

So we said, what if we turn the camera facing in? Maybe if a driver's behavior was recorded, we could change bad driving patterns and reduce accidents. Some companies invest millions of dollars in their fleets. What about taxi cabs? But the board argued vehemently against that.

Author: Based on their own assumptions of market viability...

Moeller: Right, taxi drivers drive like crazy; they don't care about safety; they don't have any money, etc. It turns out that being a cabbie is an incredibly dangerous occupation. There's a high risk of being robbed or killed. You can't get in a cab in Vegas today without a DriveCam.

Author: So did that sort of episode vindicate your approach? Did others come on board?

Moeller: No, not really (laughs). We had a lot of incredibly sharp minds, with university-type experience. Others of us enjoyed talking to customers and relied on intuition and empathy for our customers. The intuitive people debated the academics in a constructive way. We'd go and test the result in the market and they were wrong sometimes, and sometimes we were wrong.

Author: Did this affect who you brought on board the company?

Moeller: We hired and fired a lot of people who couldn't handle that startup dynamic. I once had an epiphany on the road and came back and told the company that there were going to be business plan changes. One of my executive team members looked at me with wide eyes, "but Bruce, this [the old way] is the model we have to do. You're the one who said this is how we could get there." I said, "I was wrong. I said left, now we have to go right."

Author: Is this something that can be learned; can this be taught?

Moeller: Some people apply skepticism automatically, some don't. Some can handle change, others not so much. My philosophy is you don't know what you don't know and if you were ever right in a given moment, and if your guesses were ever true it would be serendipitous. You must attack your assumptions at all times. My basic tenet: question yourself, because the world is ever-changing.

Overview

The eight steps are:

1. Document C-P-S Hypotheses

2. Brainstorm Business Model Hypotheses

3. Find Prospects to Talk to

4. Reach Out to Prospects

5. Engaging Prospects

6. Phase Gate I Compile I Measure I Test

7. Problem-Solution Fit/MVP Testing

8. Phase Gate II Compile I Measure I Test

Document C-P-S hypotheses

Objective: *You can't test your hypotheses until you create them. Write down what you believe to be true about your business idea and why it is a winning one.*

It's important to document your hypotheses by writing them down or typing them into a document. Merely storing hypotheses in your mind allows you to rationalize by altering them subconsciously to suit the occasion. Your intention is to **learn** and if you don't write them down, you impair your ability to do so. Writing down your hypotheses enables you to measure successes and failures objectively, note specific errors so you don't repeat them, and to track where you are within the process.

From the value propositions you created in the previous chapter, you will now specify your core C-P-S (Customer-Problem-Solution) hypotheses for each mission-critical entity in your business model.

Example
Paid active users:

Customer: I believe my best customers are Marketers.

Problem: They have no idea if a specific campaign is generating a return on investment (ROI).

Solution: Analytics that easily demonstrate marketing ROI.

Can you refine this? Are all marketers the best customers? Are marketers calculating ROI? Are they cognizant of the problem (is it a problem for them?) How are they trying to solve the problem today, including non-technical workarounds? How are other vendors trying to solve the problem? The objective is not to come up with phrases, but to define a hypothesis that is testable:

Customer: I believe my best customers are small and medium-sized business (SMB) marketers.

Problem: Who cannot easily measure campaign ROI because existing solutions are too expensive, complicated to deploy, and display a dizzying array of non-actionable charts.

Solution: Low cost, easy to deploy analytics systems designed for non-technical marketers who need actionable metrics.

Added bonus: These three components also serve to create your basic "elevator" pitch!

There are numerous other questions you can ask yourself to help you better understand your C-P-S assumptions. How are people dealing with the problem today? Are they using competitors? If so, why is the competition not good enough? Are people using a workaround, like spreadsheets? Or offline measures like pen and paper? What does your customer's life look like after they use your product compared to before? What is the cost of "doing it the old way?" How does it affect time, money or some sort of risk?

Example:

Current Solution: Users today have to choose between free Google Analytics or very expensive products like Omniture. Both require IT intervention and both rely on displaying "vanity metrics" such as the numbers of hits to a website or the number of unique visitors. More complicated (yet more relevant) metrics require complex website coding.

Our Solution: Our SaaS service replicates all activity on he customer's site so that it requires zero IT intervention. Our out-of-box graphs and metric tracking provides actionable, conversion-based metrics. For more complex sales funnels, our wizards walk non-technical users through funnel configuration.

Our benefits: Zero configuration saves time and money; relieves IT's headache. Our actionable metrics increase marketing ROI.

Pitfalls to Avoid
Don't be Lazy
You are NOT creating investment or marketing materials. It is imperative that you exercise discipline when answering these questions; otherwise, garbage in, garbage out. Also, it is often the case that you will present an undeniably better solution to a remarkably disinterested customer. You need to remember that humans are famously irrational. So, it doesn't matter if you are right, you must understand and describe the problem you are solving **from the customer's perspective**. When discussing how they're using the problem now, describe the specific shortfalls with the existing method. What is the cost of those shortfalls to the customer in terms of time, money, market share, risk, or customer satisfaction? Your solution must address one or more of these shortfalls. How does your solution do that? Be specific. What functionality (feature) of your solution resolves which shortfall?

Don't Mistake Guesses for Facts
You likely know what you don't know. You certainly know you need to test for those things. But you also need to test what you know you know. Those pesky "facts" you like to share about your business are likely the most significant assumptions you hold onto and are the most difficult to face head on - document and test 'em.

Exercise: explore your C-P-S hypotheses
Date of hypothesis documentation:

Draw your value chain:

Who has the problem?

What problem(s) are you trying to solve?

How are you solving the problem?

How is this person dealing with the problem now?

How is your solution better?

What benefits does the user get by using your solution instead of their existing solution or workaround?

Brainstorm Business Model Hypotheses

Objective: *Document all the assumptions required to build, market, and sell your product to the indentified customer segment.*

You have three more major sets of hypotheses to document:

1. Your business – document your assumptions concerning business model, partners, relationships, and dependencies captured in your ecosystem diagram.
2. Your product – document the feature requirements you believe are necessary to complete your final MVP.
3. Your funnel – document your assumptions about how you will acquire and convert your customers.

Business Assumptions

Return to the diagram you created in the last chapter and flesh out all of the assumptions that your diagram suggests. For example:

- My **product** reaches my customers through these distribution methods (e-commerce, SaaS, VARs, Resellers, inside sales, direct sales, etc.)
- I need to **partner** with the following companies in order to deliver a complete solution to my customer's problems
- We believe this % of free users will **upgrade** to premium accounts annually
- We will **monetize** free users via advertisers, advertising networks, data miners, lead purchasers, etc.
- Some users will pay for premium features

MVP Assumptions

Return to your Value Path diagram and document your objective for the first MVP, its "currencies," and assumptions regarding the minimum features required. If you have no intermediate MVPs, refer to your final proposed MVP. The final MVP must describe the minimum product features required that will result in each entity participating in your entire assumed ecosystem.

- Free users require these features to sign up and be active users
- What do account level 1 users require for these features to sign up and pay $x?
- Advertisers will pay $z for y # of active users/mo
- Businesses will sign a Letter of Intent based on a live demo of these features
- Strategic investors will provide development funds by proving this works in a live demo
- Users will click on the "more info" button, upon reading content of the landing page

Funnel Assumptions

A funnel represents each step a prospect goes through, from blissful ignorance to happy customer, or from Internet "Googler" to satisfied user. The first column in Figure 11 represents a traditional business-to-business funnel. You can change the labels to anything you want, but they must represent each stage a potential buyer (or user, or partner) goes through (from top to bottom), before committing to your product.

In column two, you describe your assumptions about how the customer proceeds through his or her buying decision. Note that this isn't the same thing as the selling process. The selling process is what you need to do in order to get **the buyer to do what the buyer does when he or she buys**.

Funnel Stage	Buyer's Process
Suspect	
Lead	
Prospect	
Customer	
Reference	

Figure 11: Funnel Stage and Buyer's Process

Funnel Stage	Buyer's Process	Business Task	Desired Response	Metric	Customer Discovery
Suspect					
Lead					
Prospect					
Customer					
Reference					

Figure 12: Funnel Matrix

In column 3, describe what your business must do in order to move the buyer down through the funnel. The desired action you want the user to take in response (column 4) to your activity **determines** what you need to measure (what metrics to track in column 5). Column 6 is where you brainstorm the questions you need to get answered, in order to fill out the matrix.

Example: Marketing analytics startup
Figure 13 shows a completed chart:

Read the first row from left to right:
For this marketing analytics software company, in order to acquire suspects – get warm bodies into the sales funnel – the founders are assuming that marketers are actively seeking a better marketing analytics tool. So the business task is to make their website readily available for searching and to convince bloggers who are influential among marketing analytics users to mention their solution. The desired response is for the user to click on a link that directs them to the marketing analytics' website. This can be measured by metrics such as Click-thru Rate (CTR), the number of unique visitors, amount of time on the site, etc. The last column includes questions that attempt to validate and optimize the assumptions in the previous columns.

Funnel Stage	Buyer's Process	Business Task	Desired Response	Metric	Customer Discovery
Suspect	Searching for better Marketing Analytics	SEO/SEM Social Media Influential blogger outreach	Clicks link	Acquisition (Visits, # pages, time, # clicks)	Are you actively searching for a solution? How do you research solutions? What sources influence you (mag, blog, etc.)? Do you click on ads, paid links? Referrals from friends, social networks, etc.?
Lead	Lands on SaaS Marketing Analytics Web page	Features/Benefits Messaging Positioning Case Study	Researches Download case study	Activation (Conversions, feature usage)	What do you first look for when you go to a web site to research this product? Would you like to see a video of features? Do you want to speak with someone live? Will you forward information to others?
Prospect	No risk trial convinces user to sign-up	Fully functional trial; no credit care required	Signs-up	Retention (CTR, email open rate, return visits/mo, feature usage/mo)	Do you expect a free trial? How do you feel about crippled downloads? Do you want to see a demo? Do you value white papers? Webinars? Do you require an onsite proof of concept?
Customer	Buys after 30 days of successful testing	Personalized outreach; quality support; easy purchase	Signs-up	Revenue (Conversions rate to paying, COA, LTV)	Would you be willing to pay between x & y? What shipping options are important? How important is free shipping vs low price? How important is a money back guarantee? What do you think of transaction pricing?
Reference	Tells other marketing managers at networking event	Personalized follow-up; quality support; easy reference tools	Refers other marketing managers	Referal (# referrals, referral conversion rate)	Would you like to be on our advisory board? How would you rate our customer service? Will you refer us to friends and family? Will you speak to the press on our behalf? If not, why not? What can we do better?

Figure 13: Example Funnel Matrix

Once the visitor clicks on the link (column 4), he or she becomes a lead. To continue reading the matrix, read from left to right in row 2, and so on.

Exercise: document follow-on hypotheses
Use your completed business model ecosystem diagram, proposed MVP, and funnel chart to brainstorm all of your hypotheses!

Pitfalls to Avoid
Write specific assumptions. Just about any assumption can be written so broadly that it is both irrefutable and un-testable at the same time. It is better to be wrong than vague. If you are wrong, you iterate; if you are vague, you have wasted your time and cannot draw any conclusions. For example, it's better to guess that your (initial) target market is "IT Managers in a small to medium-sized financial services firms based in Manhattan," than "IT Managers."

Find prospects to talk to

In order to test your hypotheses, you must find prospective customers to talk to. You are looking for people whom you believe are suffering from the problems you solve and who are willing to pay for (or use) your solution. In all likelihood, you cannot find these prospective customers immediately - you will have to seek them out. Fortunately, this allows you to gain experience, hone your presentation, and increase your confidence as you get closer to those people who really matter.

As shown in Figure 14, as you move toward your true target audience, your objectives of the interview become more focused.

Who you're looking for | Interview Objectives

Broad search; friends & family; LinkedIn
- Qualifying questions
- Referrals

Possible users; industry veterans
- Market insights
- C-P-S presentation feedback

Target users; early adopters
- Product-Market fit insight
- Customer acquisition

Figure 14: Interview Evolution

Depending on your business model, you may be wondering who to talk to. For example, if your business model requires you to scale users prior to monetizing them, do you talk directly to users or those who might pay for some sort of access to thousands of users? We recommend testing along the Value Path you defined in the last chapter.

How do you find and reach your prospects? There's no one right answer or magic formula. It depends on your resources, the breadth of your network, money, time, and your assumptions on how best to reach those customers. Your objective at this point is not to test customer acquisition methods, though you certainly can start to learn something about their efficacy by using them now! Here are some ideas for your initial outreach:

Exercise: Think small
Entrepreneurs think big. That's great and it is needed to be successful. However, in some instances that kind of thinking can make things more difficult. When looking for prospective early adopters to interview, you have to think small. Rather than say, "Snap! How am I going to manage to find a thousand people I don't know," think "who can I talk to about my product idea?"

Write a list of five names of people you know who share some of the characteristics (job, demographics, hobbies, industry, etc.) of your ideal early adopter customer. Log onto Facebook, LinkedIn, look at your Twitter followers, etc., and write down five names. Write an email to all five asking for introductions to five people they know, who might also share these characteristics. This is your first contact list. If you don't know anyone with the same characteristics, simply ask your network for the names of five people who might!

Pitfalls to avoid
Don't simply survey your friends and colleagues. While those people are likely to be friendly, their input is likely to be skewed. Use them to find people, not answers. Don't rely on only one method of prospect acquisition, since this will likely limit the type of person (i.e., market segment) you speak with. Experimentation may be the key to uncovering the hidden gem of who your ideal customer actually is. Also, note that these are not methods of engagement, but rather methods to obtain a list of people with whom you will engage. Don't confuse the two!

Reach out to prospects

There are several "schools of thought" regarding engagement tactics, including phone conversations, "informational interviews" and "selling before buying." The first may be necessary due to geographic constraints, but it is less than ideal, since you have no way of learning what your prospect's initial, physical, and emotional reactions are to what you are presenting. Do they flinch when you mention the price or do they roll their eyes at a screenshot? Do they begin to talk fast and lean forward? Do they bring one of their colleagues into the room to have them talk to you too? It's important to meet as many of your prospects in person as possible so that you can observe these valuable yet hard-to-quantify reactions.

"Selling before building" is a good way of learning **very quickly** whether a particular customer type might be willing to pay for your planned product. The problem with this approach is twofold: 1) you may be receiving "no sell" indications from a market that doesn't need your current problem-solution definition, but the "no" precludes you from learning where you might pivot; 2) establishing a seller/customer relationship from the get-go may limit what you can learn. A "buyer" may be less likely to give feedback about pricing, information on competitors, internal decision making processes, etc., than a "partner" who might be willing to share.

Steve Blank's formulation is geared toward creating a partner. While you eventually hope to sell to this person, the initial conversations are for learning, not selling. Steve writes:

> "Before you pick up the phone and talk to someone you don't know [assuming you get over cold call jitters], it's usually a good idea to know what you want to say. What you don't want to say is, 'Hi this is Bob and NewBanking Product, Inc., and I'd like to tell you about our new product."

Instead, you want to create an atmosphere of "needing their expertise," to which most people respond positively. The best, of course, is to be referred to someone. If you are not referred to prospects, expect to send 10 times the number of emails when you're starting out. Once you reach people you will ask for referrals, thus eliminating your no-referral problem.

You might try recording yourself or practice with friends and family.

Intro email:

Subject: Referral from {reference name}

Hi Mary,

{Reference Name} suggested I speak to you about an idea I'm working on that we hope will help marketing managers measure the return on specific marketing activities more effectively. I hear from marketing professionals that existing solutions are too expensive, too hard to deploy, and tend to display non-actionable metrics "out of the box." We hope to change all that.

{Reference Name} recommended you as a marketing executive who might have key insights into this problem. I assure you that I am not selling you anything, but rather am hoping to speak to you about this market and learn what the real pain points are.

If possible, could I buy you a cup of coffee at your convenience? I look forward to hearing from you and thank you for your consideration.

Best,
{Your Name}

Phone call:

"Hi, this is Joe at NewGeoSocNet, Inc., and as you remember I was referred to you by [insert helpful reference name here]. I appreciate you taking my call. We are starting a company to link a person's geographic location with relevant ad content on their mobile device. We are currently in the development phase and are hoping you might provide us some insight into the market. I assure you that I am not selling you anything. I would just like to understand your perceptions of the market and how you and your company target and deliver ads to mobile devices right now. In exchange, I'd be happy to tell you about some recent innovations in geo-located ad technology."

Exercise: make a cold call

You heard us. **Do it**. Do the thing you dread most: call someone you don't know and ask them about your lame idea.

What is the worst thing that can happen? They will tell you your idea is lame, that they hope you haven't quit your day job, start laughing uproariously and hang up on you.

What is the least likely thing that will happen? Oh well, they won't literally hang up on you.

But seriously, it's not like you're base-jumping off the Himalayas. Confront your fears. Make a cold call and be pleasantly surprised when it turns out people **like to share their expertise and want to help you**.

Pitfalls to avoid

Don't expect lovers, friends or family to be objective. Use them for support. For example, when you're feeling down or overwhelmed. The best practice is to just start. It gets easier once you get going.

It's amazing how easy it is to avoid "getting out of the building." Typically, several excuses are employed again and again. However, some tips for overcoming inertia include:

1. The vast majority of people are eager to help you, as long as you are respectful of their time.
2. The vast majority of people are eager to share their expertise.
3. The vast majority of people like free coffee/tea/etc.
4. When reaching out, email takes priority over phoning, because phoning prioritizes their tasks (not good).
5. Use the "Ice, Ice, Baby" presentation tips: Be Concise, Precise, and Entice.
6. JFDI!

It's worth repeating that online surveys, focus groups, user testing are not substitutes for properly conducted Customer Discovery interviews.

Engaging prospects

Problem/Current Situation/Solution Presentation

In The Four Steps, Steve Blank provides a specific method of presenting your problem-solution hypotheses. On a sheet of paper or a slide, you create three columns: one for containing the problem, another for your customer's current solution or workaround, and then your solution.

You present and discuss each column in turn, without revealing the subsequent columns. For instance, you describe the problem(s) and then get them to discuss it. Does it ring true? Do they nod? What are their thoughts on the subject? Get them to open up and talk to you about their perspective on the issue. How important is it to them? Is there a monetary aspect to the pain? The conversation should flow naturally into whether they're using a competitive product, building a solution themselves, or cobbling together a workaround. Again, you should provide leads into the conversation. For example, "I hear from a lot of CEOs that they still use spreadsheets to manage around the issue." "Who codes your online forms now? How involved is IT in deploying your current solution? Are there security issues around a web-based approach?"

Again, if all goes well, the conversation will naturally flow into your idea for a solution. This is perhaps the toughest part where it will be tough to avoid selling. Start simple. You should have your elevator pitch nailed by now. You only want to convey the "big idea" as Steve puts it, and not a list of features. Describe your core differentiator and how it is going to solve the problem. Sit back again, and look for the response. As they digest the idea, they will likely follow up with questions. The first thing you want to glean is whether they are asking questions because they don't understand, or because they are digging into the solution. If it's the former, you need to work on your "pitch." If it's the latter, you've passed a major hurdle.

The other thing you would like to discover is whether or not your proposed solution is "a vitamin or a pain killer?" (i.e., nice to have vs. must have) Put another way, here are Steve's "IPO questions;"

- What is the biggest pain about how you work?
- If you could wave a magic wand and change anything in what you do, what would it be?

As you get more comfortable with these conversations, you will be amazed at the amount of data you can uncover. Keep your broad, second set of hypotheses in mind in case these come up, or if there's an opening to bring them up during the conversation.

If you are speaking to users who you hope will pay for the product, you must frame the conversation with that in mind. If you get through 90% of the conversation and your prospect says "oh, you mean I'd have to pay?" you've just wasted a lot of time. Discussing specific pricing may or may not be appropriate, depending on your business model and what you've learned so far. We've found that open ended questions like "How much would you be willing to pay?" is a question that is often awkward to deliver, awkward to receive, and results in poor data.

Proposing a specific price or price range is better. Also, depending on how far along in the process you are, you may want to test what sort of trial would meet their expectations. For example, "If we offered a free-trial, would you be interested in signing up?"

When you close the conversation, there are several things you want to keep in mind:

- Always be gracious for their time
- If there's any fit or value you received from the conversation, ask if it's okay to follow up again later
- Ask for references for others who may be suffering from the same problem, or may have market insight
- Send a follow-up email that includes: a thank you; a summary; a list of action items, if they were created and it is appropriate; and sample text to send to referrals

Follow up email:

Hi Dave,

Thanks for taking the time to speak [meet] with me yesterday. Your insights were extremely helpful! As we discussed, here is a link to [website, presentation deck, whatever he or she was interested in seeing.] Any additional feedback would be greatly appreciated. You also mentioned that you had a couple of people in mind who might be interested in my idea or who might give me valuable feedback. I've included a blurb here for you to forward.

[blurb: {Your Name} is building a new mobile ad network linking a person's current geographic location with personalized ad content. She is looking to speak with experts in the mobile space to discuss the market and opportunities. Because of your experience in this space, I recommended she talk to you. She assures me she's not selling anything, but is merely looking for market and customer insights. Here is her contact information.]

Finally, here's the contact information for the marketing person we spoke about. If there's anything I can do for you, please do not hesitate to ask.

Best,
[Your name]

Exercise: practice your presentation

Find some friendly associates and present your problem-solution hypothesis. You're not looking for feedback on the hypothesis, but rather on your method of presentation. If it feels rough, practice. If it still feels rough, change the words in your presentation until they feel more comfortable. Use the examples here as guides, but make the words and style your own. This will enable you to feel natural when speaking with strangers. You want the presentation to be smooth so the conversation flows. Sometimes you have to learn how to get out of the way of yourself! Start by presenting in front of people you know well, but migrate to people you don't know quite as well, but whom you respect. Tell them you're looking for feedback on your presentation style but they can comment and have opinions about the hypothesis, too.

At the risk of repeating ourselves, the point isn't to practice so that your presentation comes off overly-rehearsed, but rather to be able to integrate what you need to learn it into a real conversation. You don't want the conversation to feel scripted. Through practice, you hope to find key phrases that frame the discussion and act as great on-topic conversation starters. The key is to hold onto three or four "must-learns" in your mind and steer the conversation toward learning those items.

Pitfalls to Avoid

Don't Be Knee-jerk Anti-Customer Development

Receiving negative feedback may trigger natural "anti-Customer Development" tendencies. "You just don't get it" is a common reaction to prospects who dismiss your idea. You are particularly susceptible if you do not lead the meeting. For example, the topic might wander away from the core value proposition into product features, and then possibly macro market theories. A negative reaction to one of your statements may trigger defensiveness that results in selling, rather than listening. Despite best intentions, many entrepreneurs look to confirm hypotheses, rather than test them. This is called confirmation bias and may lead to false positives.

Be Cognizant of Others' Assumptions

One thing is assured when you "get out of the building" is that people will "pepper" you with assumptions. But of course they won't be called assumptions, they will be "expert opinions" on your business model, a go-to-market strategy, company name, logo color – you name it. Take it with a grain of salt and take it for what it is: someone else's guess. Nod politely when someone asks you "have you thought of franchising?" or "have you thought of licensing your technology to Google?" It's up to you to politely steer the conversation back to the assumptions you want to test.

Phase Gate I Compile | Measure | Test

The object of the first round of interviews is to test and confirm a core value proposition, matching your product idea with a market segment that suffers from the problem you are solving. Ideally, this work occurs prior to when real product development has begun. You only begin building the product in earnest after confirming your (iterated-upon) C-P-S assumptions.

The object of the second round of interviews is to hone in on the core product functionality that your customers **must have**, while testing business model assumptions and learning the characteristics of your market segment that will allow you to reach out and acquire them efficiently. The number of interviews you conduct is dependent upon your market and nature of your interview responses. Generally, the size of your sample should be proportional to the size of your market. One could probably determine the proper sample size statistically, but that is overkill at this point. If the responses from a tightly defined segment trend clearly in one direction or another, then you probably have talked to enough prospects for this round. As Steve says, stop "when all the data begins to look the same."

Based on the interview responses, you are either ready to move forward, pivot, or you remain unclear. Responses that are all over the map likely require some kind of a pivot. For example, a modification or rewording of your hypotheses or perhaps, you simply need to speak with more prospects. If all the data is looking the same, then either:

- You have identified the right customer, who suffers the specific problem you are addressing, and who is interested in your particular solution to the problem. Once you have "discovered" your proper market segment, you are ready to start measuring product fit and to tackle your next set of assumptions. (Step 7)

- One or more of your three basic C-P-S assumptions is wrong and you must return to Step 1. Revising your assumptions may entail the following adjustments: small changes to your product idea; tweaking who your buyer might be; changes to the market segment you are pursuing; finding the exact problem you are addressing; determining your proposed solution.

Pitfalls to Avoid
Customer Feedback

One of the toughest parts of communicating with customers is knowing what to ignore and what to act upon. Again, there is no process or "Holy Grail" that will fix this for you. Intuition is an important part of being an entrepreneur. The startup founder owns the vision, the customer owns the pain. You must weigh customer input against your vision carefully. Ideally, this is why you find early adopters. You recognize an early adopter because he or she is aware of and understands the problem you are addressing, usually better than you do. This individual may already be thinking of and looking for solutions, developing one internally or perhaps has already cobbled together a workaround. When you've nailed your presentation of primary assumptions, early adopters are ready to write you a check!

How long do I have to do this stuff?

Listing eight steps in a 74 page document can provide the illusion that the Customer Development process may take merely days. This is not realistic. Customer Discovery by itself takes many months. The amount of time it takes to develop your product can be shortened somewhat via Agile development, Minimum Viable Product concepts and the like, but customer development runs in parallel with Product Development and continues for as long as Product Development, Marketing and Sales continue; for as long as the business is an ongoing concern.

Problem-Solution Fit/MVP

By this point, you have reached out to dozens of prospective customers successfully. You have also iterated (likely multiple times) on your core C-P-S hypotheses and you have reason to believe that you have determined that a viable market exists for your product. As Ash Maurya says, you have achieved "Problem-Solution Fit," and you have a strong, tested hypothesis for the right market segment.

From your many conversations, you have identified a few who are willing to work with you to further define the precise functionality of the product to suit their needs. You have also identified others who wish to track Product Development, test functionality and who are generally optimistic about its suitability to their needs. These two groups represent your "early adopters" or "earlyvangelists," as Steve calls them.

Step 7 represents a new iteration cycle, which will likely last longer than your first. During this cycle you are developing a functioning product and getting it in front of your early adopters as quickly as possible. Though your product is not highly refined, you need users to "test" your product versus their problem. This is not a classic "beta" program (though you might run one of those, too). This is not about testing for bugs or usability, but rather testing for **suitability** – are you solving the users' needs?

Circle back regularly with your early adopters, including in-person meetings. Show them or discuss your product evolution, and continue to explore the problems they are facing. Are the problems different somehow? Are they any less or more pressing? Is something else bothering them more?

If you haven't already mentioned it, talk about pricing with your customers. Before you ask how much they might be willing to pay, try to learn the **value of your solution**. It is important to remember that value is not the same as cost. Does your product save time? Money? Increase market share? Increase (their) customers' satisfaction? The price your customer is willing to pay is somewhere between what they tell you and what the real value of your product is to them.

In addition, you should be going back to your group of prospects to learn more about them as potential customers. In other words, you must validate the assumptions you documented in Step 2. From these answers, you will eventually develop a "roadmap" for acquiring and converting your prospects into customers.

Exercise: Pin this to your forehead
Am I making a product somebody **needs**?

Seriously, you need to ask this everyday - not to induce fear, uncertainty and doubt ("FUD") - but to challenge you and your team. It's not about marketing or sales or product bugs. This second iteration through Customer Discovery is all about making sure you are building something people need.

Pitfalls to Avoid
Feature Creep
Beware, you are now in feature creep danger zone. People you are speaking with are asking for different features. Some will dangle real money. It's difficult for you to say no - you have real bills. Professional services dollars are calling you, too. As you dig deeper, you discover you are serving multiple segments. What do you do?

Again, there's no one right answer. Here are some thoughts to consider:

1. You must do what it takes to keep your business alive (take consulting or custom work if you must).
2. Be committed to the vision (Don't let the lure of services income kill the product dream).
3. Choose a segment to focus on (70% resources into segment A, 20% in B, 10% opportunistic).
4. If segment A fails due to lack of size, money, or commitment – PIVOT!

Phase Gate II Compile | Measure | Test

Completing Step 8 represents the end of the Customer Discovery phase of Customer Development. You know you are ready to exit this gate when you have a strong hypothesis for Product-Market Fit based on what you've learned, as well as a representative Minimum Viable Product. Depending on your product and your business model, viability should be measured by the existence of **some amount of revenue**. Your MVP should have functionality that solves enough of your customers' problem that they are willing to pay for it. (Which doesn't necessarily mean they **have** paid, but that they are using your product with the understanding that it is a **for-pay** product.)

The next step of Customer Development is Customer Validation, wherein you start validating your customer acquisition methods (without "launching"), learn more about segments you are serving, achieve Product-Market Fit, and firmly understand your business model.

Pitfalls to Avoid
Don't take shortcuts.
All your efforts to date are rendered moot if you don't have the discipline to pivot when the market is indicating that you should. If you harbor serious doubts about anything you've learned through the course of Customer Discovery, you owe it to yourself (and any other stakeholders) to dig deeper and learn the answers to these nagging questions. Now is the time to do it!

Testing Towards a Scalable Business Model

YouSendit offers solutions for sending, receiving and tracking digital content. Ranjith Kumaran, Founder and CTO of YouSendIt.com, never thought that his early product iterations were "intermediate MVPs" per se, but they had the elements required: minimum functionality necessary to test a specific objective, based on specific user behavior. We spoke with Ranjith about how he grew the company through a series of MVPs in search of the right business model.

Ranjith discovered the pain of sharing large files due to his own frustrating experiences in various professional roles in high tech startups. As a former Engineer, Manager of Sales Engineers, and Marketing Executive, Ranjith witnessed the pain of failed attempts to send large files through e-mail first-hand. His personal experience was his primary inspiration: "If you can't get up every day and use your own product, or get up every day and see a need for your product, it's that much harder to get it off the ground."

He confirmed that others had the same needs through casual conversations (primarily) with IT people at various organizations. These were the people who were responsible for helping frustrated users exchange large files or important documents with remote colleagues, partners, and clients.

Intermediate MVP-1
Bootstrapped at the time, Ranjith and his team's first objective was to prove product viability. So they built an MVP designed to see whether anyone was interested and if so, prove their assumption that there was a viral nature to the product.

> "Our early testing included two servers, and literally a four page website – home, upload with a progress bar, upload completed, and download page. Our goal was that users would be able to browse to a file and send it to multiple email recipients within 15 seconds."

The key insight, Ranjith said, was to model their user interface after Hotwire's: "we said, 'Let's make sending large files as easy to use as booking a hotel room or finding a flight."

For their first target users, they looked for communities that would need to send large files on a regular basis: "to start, we wanted a simple value proposition," Ranjith explained. "Our first tag line was: File Too Big for Email?"

The YouSendIt team frequented message boards looking for creative professionals – photographers, videographers, anyone creating digital content – and gave them free access to their site.

The result was a resounding success. After approximately one year, YouSendIt was seeing over a million unique visitors per month! Its viral-nature spread its use beyond the creative professional, since the recipients of their file deliveries were often to clients outside of that segment. YouSendIt's traction was sufficient to raise a small sum of seed money to keep the power on and after another year, saw six million unique visits per month and based on that, closed a Series A round of funding successfully.

Intermediate MVP-2
Incredibly, up until this point, YouSendIt had no registered users! With professional money on board, however, this would soon change. Having found their Product-Market Fit with a free ad-supported product, and their subscription-based business model still on paper, YouSendIt faced the dilemma of how to best monetize their users. So they tested.

YouSendIt conducted a "bake-off" between how much ad revenue they could extract from free users versus getting people to pay.

> "The subscription model just crushed anything we could do on the ad model. The paid product was all about getting customers to pull out a credit card. Four minutes after launch [of paid features] we had a paying customer; that was the punch-line there."

From there, YouSendIt looked at pricing sensitivity, tested messaging and positioning, optimizing channels, and expanded into business segments using "secure, reliable" messaging, doubling their conversion rate. However, the pivot from free to freemium was not painless. As they concentrated on creating value for their core paying customers, they lost about a third of their traffic who decided that a secure, reliable, branded site was not what they wanted.

> "The end result today," Ranjith says, "is a more targeted, engaged 7.5 million unique visitors per month and over 12 million registered users."

Summary

In this book we aimed to articulate three levels of Customer Development thinking:

First and foremost, is the philosophy: "Be skeptical about your assumptions." In *The Black Swan*, Nassim Nicholas Taleb writes persuasively about the dangers of human beings' predisposition toward believing their own assumptions; about relying on "expert" opinions; about the appealing, albeit deceptive practice of creating narratives about the past in order to "predict" the future.

Taleb: "The narrative fallacy addresses our limited ability to look at sequences of facts without weaving an explanation into them, or, equivalently, forcing a logical link, an *arrow of relationship*, upon them. Explanations bind facts together. They make them all the more easily remembered; they help them make more sense. Where this propensity can go wrong is when it increases our *impression* of understanding."

Many business books fall into the same trap: written by experts, who create models for success based on invented narratives of past successes, completely ignoring the "graveyard" of businesses that followed the same narrative but failed.

You are already skeptical of Customer Development and Lean Startups and the slew of emerging buzzwords and supple-to-the-point-of-meaningless terms. That's great, more power to you; we applaud your skepticism. But be philosophically consistent: periodically take the time to question your own expertise and that of your friends, partners and investors. Make the effort to test your assumptions.

Second, is approaching Customer Development principles within the context of your business. For those wishing to dig a bit deeper than the philosophy, we have defined the principles and concepts, and discussed one way (there are certainly others) to think through your business model in order to help you apply Customer Development to your business. The philosophy of questioning your assumptions leads to the practice of engaging with your customers in specific ways that test those assumptions.

You "get out of the building" and test your core Customer-Problem-Solution assumptions. You define and build MVPs that test technological or market risk - the willingness of customers to pay for a specific set of features. You document and test your assumptions regarding the mechanics of your business ecosystem including the participation of 3rd party entities and the mechanics of your customer conversion funnel. You create a Value Path that attempts to create a path for mitigating high risk items first in the hopes of making major pivots as early as possible.

The third level is the step-by-step "how-to-do" Customer Discovery. For those seeking tactical guidance, we have provided detailed steps on how to work your way through the Customer Discovery processes, as well as providing context with respect to product-market fit and the other Customer Development steps. Rather than creating a laundry list of tasks or requesting answers to 100s of questions, we've attempted to "teach you how to fish" – to think about your business, document your specific assumptions, find and interview the right people and engage them in the right way, and how to recognize when it's time to move forward or pivot.

As Steve Blank says, the first step toward fundamentally changing how startups are built is to "admit the business environment is chaotic. Customer Development is a framework for operating in chaos. The objective is to see how quickly you can change guesses into fact."

We hope we have provided you a roadmap to do exactly that.

Feedback/suggestions/comments/questions encouraged.

Take or leave Customer Development. But at the end of the day (and this book), if you take only one thing away from this book, it's: "Test Your Assumptions!"

Resources

Book related

The Entrepreneur's Guide to Customer Development website (http://www.custdev.com)

Customer Development Q&A (http://questions.custdev.com)

Resources (http://market-by-numbers.com/tools_and_templates)

Brant Cooper's blog (http://marketbynumbers.com)

Patrick Vlaskovits' blog (http://vlaskovits.com)

Customer Development related blogs

Steve Blank (http://steveblank.com)

Eric Ries (http://startuplessonslearned.com)

Sean Ellis (http://startup-marketing.com)

Dave McClure (http://500hats.typepad.com)

Andrew Chen (http://andrewchenblog.com)

Ash Maurya (http://www.ashmaurya.com)

VentureHacks (http://venturehacks.com)

Cindy Alvarez (http://www.cindyalvarez.com/)

April Dunford (http://www.rocketwatcher.com)

Books
The Four Steps to the Epiphany

Crossing the Chasm

The Black Swan

Groups/Meetups
The Lean Startup Circle

Bootstrapper's Breakfast

Twitter Hashtags
#CustDev

#LeanStartups

Technical Resource Lists
Lean Startup Wiki (http://leanstartup.pbworks.com/)

Start-up Tools (http://startuptools.pbworks.com/)

Ask YC Archive (http://gabrielweinberg.com/startupswiki/Ask_YC_Archive)

About Authors

Brant Cooper

Brant Cooper is a Customer Development "practitioner," coach, mentor. If you know of a better term, please let him know. As a former Marketing and Product Management executive, he also helps high-tech companies with marketing. As a former IT guy, he helps his friends and family with computer and network problems. He blogs at Market By Numbers and lives in Encinitas, CA. He "earned" a BA in Economics from UC Davis. This is his second book, the first being a failed attempt at a novel; back in the day.

Twitter: @brantcooper

Patrick Vlaskovits

Patrick Vlaskovits thinks that Customer Development is gratifying and even fun. After reading The Four Steps to the Epiphany, he used LOIs and screenshots to validate a product idea (before writing any code) at a startup he founded and subsequently flamed out. As of late, he is back in the saddle and recently secured seed funding to test a few MVPs. He holds a Master's in Economics from UC Santa Barbara and blogs at Vlaskovits.com.

Twitter: @vlaskovits

Drop us a line. Brant and Patrick can be reached at hello@custdev.com or (415) 347-1849

Made in the USA
San Bernardino, CA
16 August 2018